Broken Silence

By Raven L. and Theo L.

Gotham Books

30 N Gould St.
Ste. 20820, Sheridan, WY 82801
https://gothambooksinc.com/

Phone: 1 (307) 464-7800

© 2025 *Raven L. and Theo L.* All rights reserved.

No part of this book may be reproduced, stored in a retrieval system, or transmitted by any means without the written permission of the author.

Published by Gotham Books (June 10, 2025)

ISBN: 979-8-3493-3514-3 (P)
ISBN: 979-8-3493-3515-0 (E)

Because of the dynamic nature of the Internet, any web addresses or links contained in this book may have changed since publication and may no longer be valid.

The views expressed in this work are solely those of the author and do not necessarily reflect the views of the publisher, and the publisher hereby disclaims any responsibility for them.

Table of Contents

Wolf and Raven 1

When Love Fades 2

Loves Gift 3

When It Comes… 4

My Apology 5

When I'm Lost 6

True love 8

Push Through 9

What To Do 10

Cursed Gift 11

As Daylight Dies 12

Insomnias' Grip 14

Pieces 15

To Dante 17

Before the Storm 18

Rain Fall 19

Bad Love 20

No More Lies 22

Behind These Eyes 23

Loves Feeling 25

Broken Puzzle 26

Dreams Die 27

Can you?	28
Oh Mother Dear	30
Beyond The Lost	31
Body of Fragility	32
Love's Dream	33
Waiting	35
For Lawrence	36
Inner Beast	38
Change	39
Guiding Love	40
Healing Alone	41
Healing Wounds	43
I know	45
Reborn	47
Give Takes Love Takes Give	48
Self-Hunting	49
Love Over Nightmare	50
Voices	52
Kiss of Darkness	53
Deep Tension	54
Blame Myself As I'm Blamed	55
Addictions End	57
Ode to Recovery	58
Grateful for Change	60
Moving Forward	62

The Lost Raven	63
Past/Present/Future	64
Lost Love Found	65
Caged Mind	67
Space and Time	68
Viewing Us	70
One Treasure	72
Nightmare Song	73
Lost Path	74
Inside My Head	75
So I Run	76
The Strongest Men	78
Desperate Prayer	79
What say you?	80
Another	81
Recovering	82
Dark Retreat	84
Someday You Will	85
The Wrath of Depression	86
Stranger to Myself	87
Take It	88
We Warriors	89
The End	90

Wolf and Raven

Wolf and Raven, soulful beings,
Symbiotic in every breath,
Wolf goes hunting, Raven follows,
One eats life, and one eats death,

Wolf and Raven seen together,
Wandering through each passing day,
Always seeking for survival,
Facing foemen along the way,

Wolf and Raven, two companions,
Facing life, two souls as one,
Wolf and Raven, side by side,
Until one's life sets like the sun,

Wolf and Raven, Raven and Wolf,
In them strength and courage lies,
Cunning through the daily mire,
Until each one of them dies.

Raven

When Love Fades

A tragic end without embrace
A fatal feeling when love fades
Tears born in eyes die on lips
Hiding them through darkest shades
Years gone by with good intent
But in the end what has it meant?
Heart is aching dusk to dawn
Fearful of emotions lent
Taken back I feel this pain
A broken heart shattered to bits
As a storm brews in my brain
And on the floor that heart sits
Pull together string to stitch
Mend the parts of what is left
Not all pieces fit together
Parts are missing caused by theft
Beating softly in my chest
Scarred and aching, held by braids
It needs comfort, needs to rest
Broken hearted because love fades…

Raven

Loves Gift

I placed you on a pedestal and to your feet I kneel.

My head stays low in awe of you to show you how I feel.

Breathing heavy and praying hard, I await your tender touch.

I sit so still and silently hope that you love me as much.

You take my hand assuring me that you'll stay at my side.

A finger gently lifts my chin and you tell me not to hide.

Stepping down from atop your perch you look to me and smile.

The air is still and motionless, we stay here for a while.

Slowly you begin to lead, you look up towards the sky.

Then you lift and stretch your arms placing me twice as high.

I turn and peak to see you kneel, now I am up above.

But you do not turn and hide your eyes, instead you show me love.

Theo

When It Comes…

When it comes, I smell the rain,
When it comes, I feel the pain,
When it comes, I see through tears,
When it comes, I'm gone again,

When it comes, I'm not surprised,
When it comes, my heart dies,
When it comes, I feel the fall,
When it comes, I dry my eyes,

When it comes, I mustn't break,
When it comes, when my heart aches,
When it comes, I must stand strong,
When it comes, for my own sake,

When it comes, my tears I'll tend,
When it comes, my heart I'll mend,
When it comes, my faith I'll keep,
For when it comes, it's not my end.

Raven

My Apology

I have to say I'm sorry, allow me to apologize.

I know that I'm not perfect and in no way wise.

I thought that I knew better, and you may have been wrong.

I guess I should know better and the truth here all along.

To speak of something as if I know when I don't have a clue,

I guess that you can expect me to act exactly the same as you.

When you know everything in the world it is hard to comprehend.

How can I stack up to you when every rule you bend.

One day I will understand what makes your mind tick.

I hope to understand one day what it is that makes you sick.

Maybe then I can truly say that I apologize.

Perhaps on that day to come I will be more wise.

Theo

When I'm Lost

When I'm lost,
I don't know what to do,
I don't know who I am,
With or without you,
I don't know who you are,
Have we even met?
I'm lost in my thoughts,
But you could have me set,
Where were you when I needed you?
Are you even real?
Everything inside of me,
Everything I feel,
It leads me straight to you,
But you don't know my name,
You've never seen my face,
And I'm dealing with the same…
I don't know your voice,
I even take a pause,
And think of how you would sound,
Saying I'm a lost cause…

Just like everyone else,

Or would you be different?

When I'm lost within my head,

Everyone is distant,

You don't even know me,

You've never heard my tears or breath,

Because you don't exist,

So I'm alone, so grant me death…

Raven

True love

As sweet as springtime rain,
As it falls from above,
As elegant as a roses scent,
Is a whispered word of love,
Adoring what could be,
Growing from what is,
Daydreams taking breath away,
A word, a hug, a kiss…
Let my love flow like a river,
Passion burning deep within,
Two hearts sing in perfect rhythm,
Letting love begin,
Will true love show in this lifetime?
No one can be sure,
But when true love makes its appearance,
Our hearts take wing and soar.

Raven

Push Through

I know that I'm not perfect, the same is true of you.
I won't stop fighting for my rights, I will just push right through.
In our time of judgement, When I find you in the end,
I will not stop, I'll keep on fighting, I'll push right through again.
Judgement comes and feelings fade, the truth I hope you find.
When that time comes I hope you know that you aren't right in mind. Reality, it may escape you, but one thing rings out true.
Noone thinking every thought will be confused like you.
When you start what you can't finish, you will realize,
Everything you thought you knew, you have built on lies.
When that time finally comes when you see the truth,
You will come to find that you have wasted all your youth.
I hope and pray that when you see, when you are not so blind,
You will start to see the truth that hides inside your mind.
Perhaps these lies will fade, you will not hide within.
We will see, in the end, if you will end your sin.

Theo

What To Do

Feeling torn in many pieces
After all that I've been through
Pushing forward without direction
Wondering what I'm to do
Pieces floating away from me
As the wind behind me blew
Holding on to what's left of me
Still I search for what to do
To my knees I drop in weakness
Lips and face slowly turning blue
Grasping to the last threads of life
Now I know what I'm to do
Fight for life Fight for survival
Feel my strength start to renew
Get up and fly now, Little Raven
Live my life, that's what I'll do

Raven

Cursed Gift

I use to feel so lost and broken until someone special came.
I realized at that very moment my life was not the same.
Peering into the deepest eyes I felt my soul at rest.
I found a meaning to myself that I did not protest.
As time goes on I find myself questioning this gift.
Slowly as the seconds tick my peace begins to shift.
As I ponder the events unfold, I begin to fear its worse.
The pleasantries that I've been given seem more like a curse.
Time ticks by and stress builds up, there is tension in my soul.
Its hard to sleep or even breathe, again opens the hole.
Emptiness is taking over, the fear has now awoken.
I am afraid the pain is back for I am lost and broken.

Theo

As Daylight Dies

As daylight dies through my hollow cries,
I mourn the death of my heart,
I scream out loud to the darkened skies,
I should have ended it from the start,
I cannot run, I cannot hide,
From the feelings of love or loss,
I wish every day to be by her side,
But her feelings confuse and cross,
Let me rend as the daylight ends,
Cleve my own flesh from bone,
Tear the skin as the night descends,
Hiding, afraid and alone,
What is love when love flees from me?
What could I have done wrong?
Rip out my heart for the world to see,
The scars that built all along,
Feast on my pain and my misery,
And I will still show love,
That is the grace that He granted me,
Unconditionally, as above…

As above, so below,

So below the earth I sink,

I reach my hand for one last hope,

My end on the brink,

Helping hands I offered out,

But this time it's me in need,

Still I fall, not knowing about,

On my pain those I helped will feed…

Raven

Insomnias' Grip

Now I lay me down to sleep and rest my weary head.

I lay awake alone at night in this cold and empty bed.

Insomnia has taken hold and strangles out my sleep.

I watch the walls as darkness falls and shadows begin to creep.

With heavy eyes that will not close I begin to go insane.

I see images of awful things begin to flood my brain.

I know in truth they are not real but illusions that will crowd.

These hateful things that let me know that sleep is not allowed.

I toss and turn, kick off my sheets and scream inside my mind.

I struggle still, hunting down the rest I cannot find.

I finally drift off to sleep, rest coming for my sake.

But it was futile, the sun now rises, it is time for me to wake.

Another restless night has passed and I am still alone.

Tomorrow is another night and I am weary to the bone.

Theo

Pieces

Pieces of my heart are scattered
Here and there, love never mattered
All the things I've done for you
Were never good enough
Say you love me, lie to me
My comforting ecstasy
When you leave my heart breaks more
Jagged edged and rough
Pieces here and pieces gone
I cannot find them, so forlorn
When the pieces turn to dust
Pieces of me die
Pieces pieces everywhere
You stole and hid them with no care
You kill me one piece at a time
I forget how to cry
This last piece I saved for you
Even with what we've been through
My love is torturing my head
This proves I'm insane

Here's the very last piece of me
Take it, look, so you can see
Once its dead I'm gone for good
Loving you in vain
This is it. What will you do?
Take it? Leave it? Crush it too?
I don't care, I'll die for you
The same way I live
There it goes, you crushed it down
Stomped it deep into the ground
Now my soulless body drops
I have nothing more to give....

Raven

To Dante

I believe that God exists, he sent me a package of joy.

He sent this very special gift in the form of a little boy.

The first thing he gave to the child was a smile like the sun.

The second thing he gave to him was a soul full of fun.

The third of the ingredients was eyes of calming brown.

When my child looks at me I can't keep feeling down.

God also blessed him abundantly with life lifting laughter.

That's the kind that lets you know you'll love him ever after.

The fifth ingredient was hair of brown to run my fingers through.

Every night I do just that when I tell him "Daddy loves you"

Theo

Before the Storm

I fear the calm before the storm,
I have been hurt and stuffed it down,
I know what comes when it's too much,
Feelings dragging until I drown,
I don't like when the storm comes,
Exploding forth from deep within,
Calamitous it devastates,
It doesn't stop once it begins,
I hold it in until it's too much,
A pit inside deeper than most,
But when the pit becomes too full,
The storm unleashed makes me a ghost,
What will come when calm is gone,
My worst disaster will unfold,
So I keep calm to keep all safe,
I lock it in with desperate hold,
I hold in more than anyone knows,
Stuffing down since I've been born,
I'll hold it in until I die,
I am the calm…I am the storm…

Raven

Rain Fall

As the rain comes falling down and pelts upon the earth,
It helps me to appreciate what all life is worth.
The softened sounds of water drops falling upon the sea,
The calming sound of impending storms help to set me free.
The patter of droplets upon this roof will bring silent dreams.
When it rains you realize life is calmer than it seems.
Standing in the water fall that nature will provide,
This is what has help me put my worries to the side.
Cold and damp I wander the earth soaked down to the bone.
I then look up to the sky and realize that we are not alone.

Theo

Bad Love

I loved you at your worst,
You loved me at my best,
I forgot all others,
You wouldn't give up the rest,
I told you I was yours,
You put me to the test,
Jealousy was yours,
While I stayed at my quest,
Be a man you said,
So I lived with a broken heart,
So many times I hurt,
Forgiving you was my art,
I wish that I had known,
You would cut me from the start,
I couldn't make you happy,
Thrown away like a dart,
You always needed something,
Love was not enough,
Always looking to be bigger,
Accepting any fake love,
But I forgave your lying ways,
And placed you high above,

So high up you buried me,

Dead inside without your love,

You held me when it was good,

But discard me for all the others,

Pretty sad, I forgave you,

For all your extra lovers,

Now it's time that I let go,

And show you the monster you made,

You turned me into a savage,

And judge me for the bed you laid,

But still you ask me for my help,

My boundaries have no grace?

You hurt me so much in life

But lie right to my face?

You shattered the heart I gave you,

Then get mad when I escape,

You judge me while I'm still helping?

What you're made of has no cape,

You're no savior with abandoned kids,

Your own cult on debate,

I'll live life with no regrets,

You messed it up, that's your fate.

Raven

No More Lies

There has been no truth here spoken, I say no more lies.
The hurtful feelings have now awoken, my spirit slowly dies.
Warning has been given out, you have not heard the cries.
Silent words of how I'm feeling sound like fading sighs.

There are no tears left behind my weary and worn-out eyes.
Tired and longing for little rest, I want no more surprise.
Caring has been strangled out, my heart shrinks in size.
Deceitful words play on deaf ears, again I say no more lies.

Theo

Behind These Eyes

I can't explain what's behind these eyes,
The torment I feel deep within,
You won't understand what caused my pain,
And I wouldn't know where to begin,
Abuse from the day I took my first breath?
Choked as an infant just because I cried?
Told I would never be anything?
Made to feel like I should have just died?
I cannot tell all my story,
Very few have witnessed my life,
I kept it a secret to protect myself,
As well as those who caused my strife,
I'll keep it inside still to protect you too,
Save you from crying and feeling sorry for me,
Because even though it hurt so much,
The love in my heart is who I should be,
I have my demons and fight my monsters,
I make mistakes and cause pain too,
But I try hard to keep them locked up,
So I can be a friend to you,

I'll keep my pain a deep dark secret,
And hide it until the world dies,
So nobody will struggle to understand,
The immense pain hidden behind these eyes…

Raven

Loves Feeling

I can't sleep when I think of you, my feelings are so strong.
I have been searching for love like yours for so very long.
When we speak I am so happy, my soul is filled with song.
When I am without your here I feel like something is wrong.
My body quivers when I dream, I am longing for your touch.
I desperately want to tell you that your love means so much.
You have been my guiding light, you have been my crutch.
Without you my life would slip just like a worn out clutch.
Stay with me and make me happy, hold me for awhile.
I have been so happy with you that when we talk I smile.
I don't want to be tossed aside like clothing out of style.
Feel my love for you that runs as long as the river Nile.
I want to fill you with this love that I hold within my soul.
Accept these feelings I thought I lost so very long ago.
I am so in love with you, as beautiful as the snow.
I want to stay with you forever and let our feelings grow.

Theo

Broken Puzzle

He's done everything he could,
Stretched himself beyond this land,
Torn his heart in more than two,
A broken puzzle becomes this man,
Put the pieces in their place,
But he will never be the same,
Now he hides behind a mask,
A broken puzzle is a shame,
He tries to smile, tries to laugh,
He cries alone without a sound,
All he wants is to be whole,
This broken puzzle...never found.

Raven

Dreams Die

I had a dream of flying high,
soaring through the light blue sky.
I peer down at the forest and stream,
Alas it is not more but a simple dream.
I had a dream of the deep blue sea,
This body of life always holds the key.
It is wonderful to dive in the water and feel,
But alas, again this dream isn't real.
I had a dream of a love so pure,
One that would not leave me broken and sore.
Love from a heart that I could not break,
But the dream ends as soon as I wake.

Theo

Can you?

Can you hear me? Can you touch me?
Can you tell my pain is real?
Can you feel me? Can you heal me?
Can you see the pain I feel?

Can you see them? My crimson tears?
Since I won't cry in front of you?
All the scars? All the sadness?
Can you tell what I've been through?

Can you listen? Understand it?
Anything that I'm about?
An "I'm Fine" tattoo also says "Save Me",
My scared tattoo is screaming it out,

No one hears my shallow cries,
I keep it all buried deep within,
Do not ask me, do not tell them,
I wouldn't know where to begin…

There is no end, there's no escape,
The hell, it haunts my dreams,
Hiding so deep, no one sees me,
When I sleep, I will not scream,

In my present and my future,
I'm always alone…
In my past I am forsaken,
And I'm never shown…

The love within is fading out,
And nobody knows I cry,
All this pain and inward hatred,
This cause of how I die,

Can you see it? Coming slowly?
Because my heart won't mend?
Can you feel it? My heart shattered?
Bringing me to my end?

Raven

Oh Mother Dear

Oh Mother dear, you've gone too soon,
much sooner than we thought.

We love you dearly and cherish
the memories of happiness you brought.

You fought hard times and many struggles to always bring a smile.

It's hard to cope without you here, but we will be fine in a while.

We will never forget your joyful laugh and the twinkle in your eye.

And though you're gone those thoughts of you will sometimes make us cry.

We realize it is not your wish to see us wallow in our tears.

It's hard to resist with all of this, you've been with us many years.

We now rejoice and honor your life, we put away our sorrow.

We live in peace and live as you did to bring a better tomorrow.

Oh mother dear, we all love you and now your pain can cease.

Move on now in the shadow of God, forever rest in peace.

Dedicated to Mom,

Love, Theo and Raven.

By Theo.

Beyond The Lost

Do you know what's beyond the lost?
The pain inside the shattered heart?
Do you know where it will end?
Do you know what made it start?
I'm trapped inside beyond the lost,
Pieces of me fade away,
Dying slowly never knowing,
If love could fix my hearts decay,
Never bending I'm always broken,
Shattered pieces drift on the winds,
Though I've loved with all that's in me,
Everyone else's love rescinds,
I'm here broken beyond the lost,
All alone lost beyond all,
Shattered me and shattered heart,
Bringing me to my next fall,
Even though I'm dead inside,
You will not see it at any cost,
Nobody will ever find me,
Alone and abandoned beyond the lost.

Raven

Body of Fragility

Ever bending, ever twisting, cellular mutation
Body burning, ever yearning to end the inflation.
Pain is swarming, habit forming fighting for a cure.
Can't believe, I feel deceived, more sorrow than before.
Never ending, mind condemning, wishing it would cease.
It's taken over, conscience holder, I feel my will decrease.
Just make it stop, I want to drop, I beg for it to end.
The next days come, and more than some I feel it all again.

Theo

Love's Dream

I had a dream I fell in love,
Safely in your embrace,
I had a dream we shared a kiss,
A smile across my face,
I had a dream of us hand in hand,
Walking down a path,
I had a dream we talked for hours,
How you made me laugh,
I had a dream we held each other,
Laying in the bed,
Watching some romantic movies,
Then I kissed your head,
I dream of how happy you make me,
Such a sweet surprise,
I dream that you say you love me,
Staring in my eyes,
When I wake it's not a dream,
This love that I feel,
When we say we love each other,
I know this is real,

I found the love I've always longed for,
Within my best friend,
I've loved you since the beginning,
I'll love you until the end.

Raven

Waiting

As I sit here facing struggles deep within my mind
Seeking out the hidden answers I cannot seem to find.
Hindered by the vicious thought of being left behind
There is no hope, I feel so tense that I cannot unwind.

Sinking deeper in dismay and filled with only doubt
The only question I seem to ask is why I go without.
Second guessing why I'm here, what is my life about?
Being trapped so deep within, I see no way out.

There is only one decision, to accept my fate.
Stuck within the pain I feel, it is myself I hate.
I held it in, by lock and key, my eyes the only gate.
But you can't see that in my soul, for my end I wait.

Theo

For Lawrence

As you leave, I wave goodbye,
Grieving, wondering, feeling lost,
Emotional I start to cry,
Saddened by the ultimate cost,
Sleep well friend, your war is done,
You fought hard and did your best,
Though your battle was not won,
You finally get a chance to rest,
I will cherish the memories,
The good times and the bad,
You helped to build the best of me,
To fight the struggles that I had,
You picked me up when I was down,
I weep for you in mourning sorrow,
What I once lost I now have found,
Your strength helps me reach tomorrow,
Someday I will join you there,
When my life comes to its end,
I'll come to the other side,
And reunite with you, my friend,

I still need time before I leave,
Because I still have work to do,
Other friends who also grieve,
But, someday, I will rejoin you,
Along with every other loved one,
Who I've lost along the way,
When my war is finally done,
I'll join you all on my final day.

Rest in peace my brother,
I love you and I will see you again in the distant future.
Raven

Inner Beast

I keep a beast caged deep within
I dare not let it out.
Buried far beneath the skin
Created with fear and doubt.
It scratches, clawing at the door
Trying to break free.
I feel it closer than before
Gaining control of me.
Crashing through the weakened bars
Fierce and filled with anger.
Lashing out, pained by my scars
Its my evil doppelgänger.
I fight to keep the beast inside
The battle has begun.
I can not say I haven't tried
But I wonder what I've done.

Theo

Change

Covered eyes don't see the truth
While open ears hear lies
Closed off minds have no perspective
They only despise
The squeaking wheel will get the oil
Open mouth gets fed
We have to change our attitudes
Not live our lives in dread
Life is how we treat each other
Emotions set aside
Open up and live life honest
Lies will not abide
Take the steps to live life better
One day at a time
Listen to a better option
Than to live in crime
Times get hard but they get better
It's about how we live
When we change our way of thinking
Love is what we give

Raven

Guiding Love

Words simply can not express the way you make me feel.

Yearning for the sense of love, one that didn't seem real.

I prayed for someone just like you to save me for so long.

Then an angel sent my way touched my heart with loves song.

Through dark times when I felt weak, you became my light.

When I was down and couldn't go on, you gave me strength to fight.

You lit the path in front of me and helped me see the way.

I move forward with thoughts of you helping me every day.

I know my place is beside you, my life is finally right.

I await your tender touch and to lay with you at night.

My heart aches without you near, what saves me is your love.

I'm thankful to the heavens for you, my angel from above.

Theo

Healing Alone

I'm learning to heal with a heart wide open,
But it's hard to love when my heart sits broken,
Suffering alone becomes my burden,
I won't drag anyone down with me,

I'm learning what I want in life,
I'm trying hard to be alright,
I learn alone I have to fight,
I'm alone trying to be free,

Nobody cares when they see my pain,
They judge and criticize, call me insane,
They hate me for all my scars,
Though many scars they can't see,

In my head memories of hurt,
Wishing six feet in the dirt,
Failed attempts to leave this world,
Please just leave me be,

Finding someone who understands,
But loves me anyway because they can,
I don't know if I can find it,
Dreams versus reality,

So I try to heal alone,
In this world as cold as stone,
Telling nobody how I feel,
For fear it will make them flee…

Raven

Healing Wounds

I use to cut myself and watch it bleed,
Borderline suicide that couldn't succeed.
The physical pain was better to feel
Than the emotional emptiness I wish wasn't real.
I'd get lost in the sorrow and sadness I felt
Not knowing how to cope with the pain I've been dealt.
I'd hide what I've done with shirts of long sleeve,
Saying "I'm fine" for peers to believe.
When caught on occasion I'd say "it was my cat",
Most people would tend to believe when told that.
But I owned no furry feline companion,
It was my knife I would cut with, emotions abandoned.
One day another noticed my deep scratches
And said signs like those, their attention it catches.
Showing me theirs that were from their feline,
They said theirs were different and looked nothing like mine.
They then grabbed my hands and stared into my soul,
They knew, they could see that I had no control.
I soon broke down and told the secret I kept,
I spoke of my depression as I sat and I wept.

I learned on that day to speak up when I'm sad,
If not I would die by the pain that I had.
The scars have healed over after all of these years,
But secretly I still see them, my pain and my fears.

Theo

I know

I know that you feel all alone,
You've endured much grief and pain,
Maybe forgotten what you're worth,
And feel like there's nothing to gain,
Your thoughts always torment you,
And put your body through such strain,
You don't know who to turn to,
You don't want to trust again,

You feel lost within yourself,
Wondering why you've been so blind,
All the love within your heart,
Wasted on those who were not kind,
So you separate yourself,
You get trapped within your mind,
I'm not like anyone else,
I will not let you fall behind,

I know these things because we've talked,
You're not alone, I feel it too,

All the sorrows of your past,
I feel it, that's what I've been through,
Come take comfort in my arms,
I won't stray away from you,
Real knows real, we've seen so much,
I know, you know these words are true.

Raven

Reborn

I felt the sun for the first time, but I don't mean on my skin.

I left the warm rays shining down penetrate within.

Realization is not my strength on most of my aware days.

But for some odd reason, today is different in many ways.

I felt revived, more alive, more of what I use to be.

I felt restored, kind of reborn, with open eyes that see.

Too many times I ignored the truth, I ignored the signs.

I focused on negativity, used depression as my binds.

Before I knew it, I was always sad, ignoring the warmth of the sun.

I alienated myself from friends and family, withdrew from everyone.

But today is different, I don't know how.... But I feel so blessed.

I put away the past that defined me and laid sadness to rest.

I hope that this can be an inspiration to any other lost souls.

Those that live in fear, in hiding, because they have no control.

We can move on, beyond our past and see how strong we've become.

I've realized it takes much less to see how much we have won.

Theo

Give Takes Love Takes Give

Take a stand, take a glance,
Take a moment to understand,
Take your feelings, take a chance,
Take the risk to take a hand,
Make a choice, feel the rain,
Make a wish to make change,
Take it in, feel again,
Take a step to explore the strange,
Fill your soul, fill your heart,
Choose to love the life you live,
Live and love, a work of art,
You get what you give.

Raven

Self-Hunting

Stuck inside my head again, on the wrong side of the tracks.
The voices circle, surrounding me like ravenous wolf packs.
It seems to me there is no escape no matter how hard I try.
    I need to make a break for it, for if I don't I'll die.
    I have tried, quite feebly, to find a place to hide.
But no matter how secluded, these thoughts don't subside.
    Being alone and isolated only seems to make it worse.
    Why, I ask to no avail, am I stuck with this curse?
In honest belief I begin to think that I just can't break free.
Maybe I'm wrong and all along the wolves were really me.

            Theo

Love Over Nightmare

Ghosting mostly all around me,
Take this time to keep me grounded,
I see pain in my reflection,
But those closest see me rounded,
Hiding tears behind a smile,
Holding on a little while,
But alone I let the pain flow,
Crying, feeling infantile,
Let me sleep away my dreary,
Haunting dreams leave me so weary,
But it beats my reality,
Waking up seems even more scary,
Touch the blade of my own nightmares,
Wondering why I can't stay here,
Cut the cord of lucid moments,
Numb myself from those who don't care,
Leave a world with memories fleeting,
Fade me out, my soul is pleading,
These thoughts when I'm stuck in limbo,
My emotions so defeating,

Let my light burn out forever,

Never waking, I surrender,

Then I here "I love you, don't leave",

The cries of "I want us to stay together",

Snap back to the present moment,

I can't ghost her, loves component,

Look around, dazed and confused,

The nightmares are my worst opponent,

I know where my heart belongs,

With one who forgives all past wrongs,

Ride or Die because Real Knows Real,

Is this a dream or love true song?

Raven

Voices

Stuck inside my head again, I can't seem to understand.

I want to break but I just bend, the voices strong demand.

Tell me how to silence them, there's no way to break free.

They whisper, calling my name again, so much tension inside me.

There's no way to break this hold, it's driving me insane.

No matter what, it makes me fold, everything is in vane.

I guess they get to win tonight, their only motive is sorrow.

I can't give up even though I might, I hope they are quiet tomorrow.

Theo

Kiss of Darkness

Hello Darkness, my old friend,
You've come to take my soul again,
Rip and tear my sinew and bone,
For all my pain that you have sewn,
Bleed me out to my last breath,
Bring it close, I'll embrace death,
Lay me down at last at peace,
End the pain of which you feast,
All alone no one will cry,
When I finally say goodbye,
This painful fate I will abide,
With your assisted suicide,
You swallow me in cold embrace,
And shove my dead heart in your case,
Lay me down when I am gone,
So those who hate me can move on,
Never to know true loves bliss,
I settle, instead, for your deadly kiss…

Raven

Deep Tension

Shadows keep surrounding me, the secrets that they hold.
So many things I should acknowledge, those words left untold.
The darkness that I feel I'm under, everything feels cold.
My sight is drifting, ever watching, no beauty to behold.
The air is heavy and stifling, I find it hard to breathe.
I feel it deep like lungs collapsing, so hard to believe.
Gasping deeper, almost choking, no oxygen received.
I had hoped it would be easy, now I feel deceived.
Passing out, I feel so lacking, with tension in my chest.
I'm giving up, I know it's over, there was no contest.
Laying here I realize that it may be for the best.
I really wish this was the end so I could forever rest.

Theo

Blame Myself as I'm Blamed

What would I give up?
I'll give up everything,
To not feel alone,
To not feel that pain,
I've known it many years,
I don't want it again,
I want to feel something,
Love that's not insane,
Kindness that's not fake,
Accepted as I came,
Dark but loving anyway,
Why have I been shamed?
Walking all alone,
These dark woods feel the same,
I cannot see the moon I love,
Am I the one to blame?
Leave me hollowed out,
As a husk of former game,
Hunted by the ones I loved,
Slaughtered, beaten, maimed,

Like a lone wolf I survive,
Nobody knows this name,
Even after the love I've shown,
I'm still alone to blame…

Raven

Addictions End

A new day and a brand-new start.
I'll take this opportunity straight to heart.
My thoughts always wandered, not very smart.
I've let my addiction tear my family apart.
Now begins treatment, not just for myself.
I do it for everyone who said I need help.
I'll place my addiction on an unreachable shelf.
This is my chance to restore my health.
With everyone watching, today I begin.
I'll keep one foot forward, put an end to my sin.
There's no giving up to find peace within.
With determination, with strength, I can win.
Goodbye addiction, you've hurt me too much.
With my loved ones beside me, I leave in a rush.
My mind and my body, you'll no longer touch.
I turn my back to you, now silence, now hush.

Theo

Ode to Recovery

I feel at home trapped in the chaos
I feel alone inside this hell
I put on a big fake smile
I tell everyone I'm well
I'm not ok trapped in this torment
I just want to numb it out
So I turn to what I'm used to
This is what it's all about
Selfishly I drink that tonic
I can feel it wash away
All the sickness and the anguish
Til it comes back the next day
Something harder, something deadly
That is what I really crave
Something sickening numbs everything
To my demon I will cave
Bend me break me I don't mind
I'll use it as an excuse to go
Next time more times every kind
I use everything I know

Numb this sickness til I don't hurt
That's the sweet spot best unsaid
Anything that I can do
To get myself out of my head
But it hurts the ones around me
So what, I'm still seeing red
Just a little more to calm me
But the shame is I'll end up dead
Gotta change this hell I'm living
I can't take my brain no more
I get thinking and it hurts me
Why I'm this way, I'm unsure
But I need to find the answer
So I can l change the way I think
If I don't do something different
I'll end my life with drugs and drink

Raven

Grateful for Change

I'm grateful just to be alive
When everything feels wrong
I cannot give up this fight
Forcing my way along
Grant me the serenity
To accept what I can't change
This is something hard for me
This concept seems strange
Also grant me the courage
To change what I can
Change the way I look at life
To be a better man
Finally grant me some wisdom
To know which one is which
What I can change and what I can't
Time to make a switch
I've come so far but have far to go
This fight is never won
But I can finally change my life
The old me is done

I'll lose some people along the way
But I will be alright
I finally have new found strength
To fight this endless fight
I can love myself today
I've never been so sure
I now have a self-respect
I never had before

Raven

Moving Forward

My anxiety is slowly rising, I don't know what to do.
The path ahead is so surprising, so much to go through.
I admit there is a fear, it's too great to ignore.
I'm missing something I held dear, I'm lost and ask "what for"?
In a place that was my heart, there now resides a hole.
I feel my world torn apart, inside me, an empty soul.
My steady hands now only shake, I can not hold them still.
Activities that I partake, I struggle to find the will.
I'm trying hard to move along, at least that's my intention.
But there are still many things wrong, so much pain to mention.
It seems I'm still set in depression, I guess I need more time.
I'm slowly counting down the days to the mountain I must climb.
I take a breath, breathe in deep and walk towards my destination.
As I go I will not weep, I pray it's not devastation.
There must be better things for me, I say in contemplation.
It's brighter sky's I wish to see, I need a positive revelation.

Theo

The Lost Raven

Closed off to reality,

Your words fall on deaf ears,

Closed in your insanity,

You ignore all of your fears,

I could not save you from yourself,

Beautiful disaster,

You tried hard in every way,

To make yourself my master,

Damage me, break my heart,

Tell me I can't be loved,

But it's you suffering all alone,

Giving in to lust,

My heart lay shattered on the floor,

Lost Raven, a casualty of you,

But now I'm stronger so I'm thankful,

For all you've put me through…

Raven

Past/Present/Future

They say the past is history and quite often forgotten

We push bad memories aside because they seem so rotten

Those memories push to the surface when we are in doubt

The painful things we bottle up because we did without

They say the present is a gift, it is something we pull near

A lesson or time with friends and loved ones is something to hold dear

We need to make these memories and place them in our heart

We'll hold onto these "histories" so we don't fall apart

The future is a mystery as far as we are told

We do not know what to expect until the dice are rolled

The future will be present, a gift yet to receive

You can take ahold of it as long as you believe

There are many things to gain, through darkness they will shine

You must take ahold of them and claim "these things are mine"

Theo

Lost Love Found

I've loved and lost, I've let it go,
And felt such pain, Some never know,
All that I've done, To help them grow,
And all I received, A hurtful blow,
I have not lost, There's love in me,
I show the world, My heart on my sleeve,
A shattered heart, For all to see,
Broken pieces, This shouldn't be,
Devastated, I walked alone,
Just as before, It's all I've known,
After everything, The love I've shown,
But me being loved, No one can condone,
I sit here crying, With the pieces of my heart,
Stitching them together, My ugliest art,
I wish I had left, Long before the start,
But the love in me, Won't let me depart,
So I hold on, Praying to find love true,
I don't want to feel dead, I don't want to feel blue,
I want that embrace, I want to get that clue,
It's in my head now, You said "I love you"

I feel that sting, The fear creeps in,
But I feel it inside, New love begins,
I've known for years, Where my heart has been,
You know my pain, You know my sins,
But you love me, With all my flaws,
I'm here for you, Whenever you call,
We pick each other up, When one of us falls,
No matter how long, I'll give it all,
Take all my pieces, And I'll take yours too,
We'll fix it together, What we've been through,
If you'll be mine, I'll belong to you,
Because this love feels right, Because this love feels true.

Raven

Caged Mind

As I lay here trapped in sorrow,
Thinking there is no tomorrow.
Biding, finding not but pain,
None to lose but none to gain.
Am I simply sitting here,
Emotionlessly facing fear?
Staring at the cold dead walls,
Echos screaming down the halls.
Pale light shining through the glass,
Seconds tick as time does pass.
But time stands still, I've come to find,
Trapped inside my cage like mind.

Theo

Space and Time

Space and time are mine alone
Nobody else can call this home
In the end I suffer my fate
All alone for you to hate
Send your dreams and fears to me
Where nobody else can see
I alone will bare the shame
Left alone in constant pain
For I alone can take the dark
Leave me here with scars to mark
All my suffering comes undone
When at last you say you won
All the sorrow and sadness
Leaves me in a state of distress
But a burden you can't take
Is mine alone as you forsake
Constant drowning misery
Mine alone to your ecstasy
Love your life in happiness
While I suffer in loneliness

Smile your joys as I fade
And take all of your pain away
Live your life of constant crime
While I dissolve in space and time

Raven

Viewing Us

How we view ourselves is tragic
Confidence or despair
Like drowning in a sea of sorrow
Fighting to get air
We take all of it to extremes
Are we right or wrong
We need to find a healthy balance
And learn to get along
Compromise can take us so far
But nobody sees
We can find a way around it
Or just leave it be
What we chose affects us greatly
Positive or not
If we act out incorrectly
Our souls seem to rot
Embrace change and find that middle
Let's show ourselves some grace
So when we look in the mirror
We don't have to brace

Face ourselves with good intentions
As we should with others
Show love, peace and harmony
To our sisters and brothers
I hope we can change the way
We view everything
So we love ourselves and others
Togetherness we'll bring
I will leave it on this note
And it may seem strange
Let us find a new perspective
Let us be the change

Raven

One Treasure

Of all I've lost, I still have one, the thing that keeps me strong.

A single solitary treasure, the right when all is wrong.

It beacons out among the silence, echoing its song.

When everything was lost or broken, it stayed all along.

If I'm lost within my darkness, it shows me the light.

It guides me gently on my path when blindness takes my sight.

It is the sun that frees my soul from everlasting night.

When I feel like giving up, it gives me strength to fight.

My treasure musters motivation when I think I'm done.

If I falter, falling over, it picks me up to run.

Of all majestic in the world, it is the only one.

The thing that truly keeps me going is my loving son.

Theo

Nightmare Song

Sorrow drenched with nightly sweat,
Nightmares of a damaged soul,
Beating heart be still no longer,
Pulsing out of my control,
Wake me from this maddening slumber,
Screams that cannot leave my lips,
Reach before I'm torn asunder,
Hanging on by finger tips,
Letting go of controlled chaos,
Unchained inner rabid beast,
Woken from its dreamy status,
Ravaging who expects it least,
Wake me from this morbid nightmare,
Send me off on silver wing,
Do not let my conscience die here,
Lift my heart and let it sing.

Raven

Lost Path

I try to walk the beaten path but end up all alone.
Seeking comfort everywhere but I am on my own.
Tension builds up, deep inside, trapped in the unknown.
There seems to be no exit out within the overgrown.
Abandonment has come for me and begins my desolation.
I try to take control of a most dire situation.
But, in my lack lack of confidence, find only hesitation.
There is no hope for me, I fear, in strifing desperation.
I wish I could go back and change what made it all begin.
But now I find that I'm trapped here, struggling within.
A sorry soul, a poor excuse, a burden I have been.
I must find solace in solitude to which I am akin.
It's so strange how, when all alone, no one seems to come.
Or how they judge when they don't care what hell you just from.
They don't see that deep within I am stagnantly numb.
They can't feel the deep despair to which I will succumb.
I should have known that all along things would end this way.
Feeling lonely, lost and broken has left me in dismay.
I want to move beyond this path but feel that I must stay.
And so I sit here quietly, waiting to decay.

Theo

Inside My Head

Caught inside a tangled web
Despair, lies, and deceit
Hoping I can break away
The cycle on repeat
Inside my head I'm locked away
Afraid and alone
Prison bars won't let me out
Cold as winter stone
Pray for me that I survive
Though I feel already dead
This is what it's like for me
Stuck inside my head…

Raven

So I Run

I can no longer cry. My eyes are bloodshot red.
I cannot stand these awful thoughts that swim inside my head.
Round and round they go. They do not seem to cease.
If only I could make them stop and once again feel peace.
They do not come and go. They remain persistent.
Someone please take them away and end my pain this instant.
I do not wish to care. I no longer want to feel.
I am in isolation during this desperate ordeal.
Insomnia returns. I cannot seem to sleep.
I lay awake alone at night and only seem to weep.
A blanket soaked with tears.
The mattress feels so cold.
I stay like this for I am one that no one wants to hold.
Does anybody care? I do not think they would.
So I keep everything inside because I feel I should.
I wish to disappear. As a shadow I will roam.
I won't be missed by many since I feel I have no home.
Will I be remembered? Or forgotten when I'm gone?
These are the only thoughts I ponder as my life moves on.

Maybe I'll return one day. I can't say if or when.
So take these final words from me, "Until we meet again".

Theo

The Strongest Men

Feeble fable, this strong willed man,
Dying inside he cries at night,
All alone doing all he can,
Telling everyone that he's alright,
He feels lost when thoughts flood in,
Is he doing enough for them,
His feelings stuffed inside his chest,
To the darkness he feels condemned,
A good man fights to provide a home,
And show love he does not get,
So his thoughts will race and roam,
But he fights on so they are set,
All alone he cries his tears,
Hiding so no one can see,
And the thing that hurts the most…
Realizing this man is me…

Raven

Desperate Prayer

Lord above, I'm feeling lost and so I kneel to pray.

I close my eyes and fold my hands but don't know what to say.

Within the silence I begin to seek deep in my soul.

I have unanswered questions that have left a blackened hole.

Inside this hole I am too blind to see your guiding light.

And so I ask of you to grant to me your blessed sight.

Offer me your hand to hold and guide me as I walk.

When I cannot find the words, encourage me to talk.

Embrace me deep within your arms as I make my confession.

Dry my tears and heal my heart as I speak of my depression.

In the name of your loving son, I hope you hear my plea.

And so I end, with an Amen, my prayer from bended knee.

Theo

What say you?

What say you when you're afraid?

Let me lend an ear.

What say you when you're in pain?

Let me wipe your tear.

What say you when you feel alone?

I'll be a friend to you.

What say you when your scars are shown?

I will show mine too.

What say you when you are down?

May I lift you up?

What say you when you thirst for life?

Can I fill your cup?

What say you when you're in need,

And I offer my hand?

Will you share the same love as I?

Together shall we stand?

Raven

Another

Another day, another lie.
Another hour ticking by.
Another question, I wonder why.
Must I make another try?
Another drink to drown my soul.
Another choice to lose control.
Another death, another hole.
Another loss yet takes its toll.
Another smile faking grace.
It rests upon another face.
Another dream to try and chase.
It pulls away in another race.
Another story to be told.
Another speaking, acting bold.
Another night shivering cold.
Alone without another to hold.
Another quickly answered call.
Yet another ignored by all.
Another attempt to stand tall.
But I trip in another fall.

Theo

Recovering

Trauma of the past does hurt,
Even more when done again,
Loosing sight of who I am,
Trying to stay on the mend,
Day by day I find my strength,
And give a caring ear to lend,
Knowing any given moment,
Drama can begin again,
Still I walk my head held high,
Ready to be someone's friend,
Until I hear those words that cut,
That tear, that rip, that stab, that rend…
Pick myself up from the bottom,
Why do I let myself fall?,
I can't let this go on longer,
With my back against the wall,
I step forward not defeated,
I know that I must stand tall,
Show no fear to my past demons,
Or that fear I can recall,

My recovery was not easy,

My traumas I still can see,

All the pain, the hurt, the sorrow,

It still lives inside of me,

But today I don't surrender,

To temptation haunting me,

I have found a way to change it,

Found a way to be set free.

Raven

Dark Retreat

My head may be the darkest but the safest place I've known.
I know that it's not perfect but at least it is my own.
Sometimes I get lost within as I wander and I roam.
I run and hide inside this darkness, making it my home.
I only struggle in this place because there's no way out.
It keeps me safe from all the things I know nothing about.
The world, filled with pain and sorrow, is no place to be.
The saddest part is it's the same, this darkness inside me.
Deeper, darker, into shadow, until no light I see.
I built my cage inside this place so I am never free.
People say it isn't safe to be stuck in my mind.
I get trapped inside this crevice, the darkness they can't find.
I keep going, deepest, darkest, with no light to be shone.
I wonder if I prefer this place where I am all alone.

Theo

Someday You Will

Someday you will have a heart,
Someday that heart will break,
Someday you'll understand,
Someday you'll regret mistakes,
Someday you'll be left alone,
Someday you'll be afraid,
Someday you'll see it all,
Someday you'll see what you made,
Til then I will pray for you,
Afterwards I will as well,
I don't want you to know,
What it's like inside my hell.

Raven

The Wrath of Depression

Alone I stand close to the ledge,
Feeling dead inside,
I step closer to the edge,
I can't run or hide,
I feel it calling out to me,
I take another step,
A bottom that I cannot see,
Remembering tears I've wept,
Closer, closer, just one more,
Emotions will not bend,
Falling to that rocky shore,
Soon it all will end,
I want to fall, I don't want to,
I feel torn in half,
Insanity I'm going through,
My depressions wrath.

Raven

Stranger to Myself

I don't know me anymore, I think I've run away.
My sanity slips through the cracks as I plead for it to stay.
Tomorrow will be far too late, I must be found today.
But I've gone and left myself, I've begun to stray.
When I look into the mirror, it's not me I see.
I've gone and left a mental note for myself to leave me be.
There is a secret place I know where I sometimes feel free.
Just let me go, I tell myself, making my last decree.
I stand staring as I watch myself walk out the door.
I'm going to that place that I have never seen before.
I know that I have built this place of solitude galore.
My palace of loneliness that I seem to adore.
I reach and beacon to myself as myself says goodbye.
I beg myself to please return as I sit and wonder why.
I cannot say I love myself because it is a lie.
I am a stranger to myself and no longer care to try.

Theo

Take It

In this world I give so much,
I take so little and I'm out of touch,
I live a lonely reality,
My heart in my hand for the world to see,
Take a pill to take a fall,
Take a drink to forget it all,
Everything I can recall,
The pain within isn't so small,
You'll see me smile because I'm fine,
But deep inside I wanna die,
What's the point of my madness?
It's a way to hide my sadness,
I'll take this blade across the skin,
Or you'll take it from me before I begin,
Yes or no, should I be saved?
Or to my demons stay enslaved?

Raven

We Warriors

In a world where I'm condemned,
I always try to make amends,
I make right sins not my own,
My existence is not condoned,
Ashes of a shattered heart,
Blown away before my start,
But still I stand up proud and tall,
Showing love to one and all,
We may be broken, hurting curs,
But we fight on, as warriors.

Raven

The End

My heart is shattered, pieces scattered, never to be whole.
And with its breaking, ever shaking, lies my empty soul.
Pain has mounted, mind is clouded, will I ever cope?
I grab my knife, devoid of life and slowly losing hope.
Crimson bathing, steel blade scathing, just to feel alive.
But isolate and desecrated, how can I survive?
I'll lay to rest by carving flesh and cleaving to the bone.
Save your sorrow for tomorrow when I make death my own.
Torn asunder, buried under wicked means again.
I'll take my place in deaths embrace, welcoming my end.

Theo

www.ingramcontent.com/pod-product-compliance
Lightning Source LLC
LaVergne TN
LVHW031614060526
838201LV00065B/4831